FANTASIES AND FOIBLES.

By

Jennifer Lee Wilson

"Illustrated by Judy Tamagno"

I

Passion for Publishing

Your

Written Words

Website: www.pfppublishers.com

Email: www.p.f.p.publishers@gmail.com

8

©2008 Passion for Publishing Publishers.
Book manuscript & interior design by Pat Simpson.
Cover and interior illustrations by Judy Tamagno
ISBN 978-1-4092-4580-3

Contents Page One

Contents Page Two

Contents Page Three

ACKNOWLEDGEMENTS

First and foremost
I want to thank my lifelong friend,
Judy Tamagno.
An accomplished professional artist in her own right.
Without the loan of her tremendous talents
covering and illustrating my book
and her constant support, I would be lost.
I also wish to thank Pat Simpson
for her kindness and expertise,
for surely this book would never have happened
without them both.

Dedication

This book is dedicated to my family and friends

I write because I enjoy it,

to express all human emotion,

for love of the English language

and mostly because

I must.

JLW

The Prince of Words

You are the prince
of ponytails and ribbons
with bare feet chasing rainbows

you are the prince
of first sighs and giggles
of moons and swoons dreams

you are the prince
of white veils and bouquets
and happily ever promises' sureness

the prince of oceans
that ebb and flow and rage
with all the powers of Poseidon

you're prince of tears
whenever tragedy cuts deeply
cruelly without thought or reason

your only domain
is the world of words
and within it you are the prince

Words - Do it For Me

Reality, I'm so tired of you.
Sick of crying, sick of bills.

I want words that rock my world,
make stars shine and vines entwine,
make the poets' inkwell spill,
do everything they can and will.

Words, do your finest magic,
take me far away from it all.
To softest sandy, sun warmed beaches
with glittering clear insect chirped nights,

Hearing rhythmic bongo slaps
and feel as warm water laps
around and between every toe.

Words, I beseech thee,
do this for me, set me free
Send me to a place where anything goes.

Dragonfly

Fairies exist in the vaporous mist.
From whence did they come to so shyly hide?
Answering lies in times hazy, years kissed,
Forgetting when dragons and wizards allied.

Faeries then had no wings fearing greatly.
A kindly wizard appeared, saw and wept.
The faerie queen observed chaos stately
and quietly shed a tear which she kept.

Distressed she watched her subjects run quickly,
dragons and wizards together did prance.
'Oh kind force above', she whispered thickly,
'how can I help them stop this deadly dance'?

Wizardly hearing her thoughts, 'what can I do'?
Sending a message upon gentle breeze,
he sent her answer on wishes that grew
larger as she shouted, "do it soon please"!

The wizard said 'there is power in tears',
so let's combine ours and see what transpires.
From single drops grew a babe with no fears
because it had wings to fly from the fires.

Soon faeries had wings and dragons were gone,
faerie queen breathed easy, said with a sigh,
'with each faerie wing a dragon begone',
and in each place, grew a sweet dragonfly.

Forest Refuge

I take refuge in this strange grove,
shut my eyes and wish dearest wishes.
Whisper sweetest words as breezes rustle,
shade twining vines from glowering sun.

Wither not, vast trunk from
whence comes tender branches.

Be my sanctuary, be my haven
in this singular magical grove
where flowing rivulets bubble merriment.

Summer warmed stone observes
and you my dearest,
reveal not this enchantment.

Forest goddess hear my wishes,
show your face
hear the woods murmer, hear me.

Your presence bestows grace,
here I am beauty.

Morning Thoughts

I woke with an epiphany,

an understanding, a clarity

of thought heretofore beyond

my understanding, and I

floated through my day

secure in the knowledge I

had unlocked one of the secrets

of my existence,,,

then I tried to remember,

huh?

I hate when that happens!!

Summer's End

Can anything be sadder than late summer?

Were days ever so golden, clear-eyed and unending?

Was love ever so deep, with infinity standing before us?

Is it all seen through the kindness of gossamer haze?

Memories of what was is still in full evidence

but the freshness is long gone.

Drooping has begun, gray is creeping in.

Lack of rain causes ground to crack, and

what happened to dewy spring?

It seems only hours ago.

But Autumn has it's own charms,

it's own rewards.

And so we tell ourselves

as we walk down the avenue,

ignored.

Smoke and Mirrors

It's an illusion
a trick of the eye
sleight of hand
made in mists of the mind
just outside
the edge of the mirror
made with
stinging smoke and a
tear

fumes escaping the hidden
trapdoor
ALWAYS
there making the
disappearing act
painless and not obvious

but to whom is it not
painfully obvious
to whom is it
illusion
and not real?

Absence

Why has such a painful hole

opened up my being?

It's because of

silences,

things that weren't said,

should never be said

but their absence nonetheless pains.

What was said

wasn't finished,

truths unrevealed , half-done,

surrendered to forced abandonment

once again.

The Curse

Counted at last, my life was my own,
friends I had, faces and places I'd see
Along came one, saying "Hi, how are you?"
For a while he and she, then two ones were we.

You would remember the sweet endless days,
restaurants, the concerts, the places we went.
You would remember the starlit splashed nights,
ice cream sodas, the parks, wishes we sent.

You would remember long drives and travel,
deep conversation saying, "Yes, I do care."
You would remember us acting like kids,
the movies, the fairgrounds, the plans we'd share.

It's not five years since your ashes were strewn,
your pain finally gone, your soul at last free.
I am cursed with rememb'ring two thousand days
about you and me, when two ones were we.

There You Sit

There you sit, that gleam in your eye,

staring that well known hole through me,

knowing how I look in the tub,

with me each morning as I wake.

Old memories speak as I watch,

saying things I don't dare confess,

after smelling the scents of love

falling into my bubbling bath

.

You tasted every tear shed

heard each whispered vow and promise,

seeing every shattered dream

my only love, my teddy bear.

Little Miss Perfect

Little miss perfect slipped into a town

she was everything expected of her

don't you dare weep or express anger deep

don't you laugh just smile

miss perfect became stricken deathly ill

abused while half dead by doctors on call

afraid to speak, that was not expected

don't you weep just smile

recovered body but trauma inside

forget, don't tell and that's what's expected

she swallowed those nasty little green pills

and laughed and screamed loud

Love Me True

Love me not for nature's mistake of face,

love me not for the smile when I see thee.

Pray love me not for my blushing embrace,

or for crimson cheeks at a moment's glee.

Please do not love for sweet words sown in May,

or fully formed blossoms of latest June.

When winter's rages become rulers of day,

Love me truly as in summertime's swoon.

Thy visage, thy frowns be bits of thine soul,

Dearest be each and every small part.

Love me by half as I treasure each toll

Of the bell chiming on each side of my heart.

I ask devotion as golden sun sets

And as much of thee as thine spirit lets.

A Knight's Beginning

A man awakened in dawn's dewy mists
thrown far by foolish enchantment and spite.
He knew not who and from whence came his lists
of duties and trials that would test his might.

Genevieve gathered flowers by pale light
screamed fear as the shadow of man on her fell.
"Who are ye and why have ye come to my sight"?
"I know not, mayhap be under a spell."

They spoke of many wonders they didst see,
she saw so noble a visage twice pure.
"I dub thee Sir Andrus whilst here thou be"
he arose feeling whole and very sure.

Then on blossomed mutual attraction
followed thus by complete captivation.

A Knights Return

Returned from enchantment and mystery
unable to forget his flaxen haired maid,
the knight rememb'ring flames of ecstasy,
wandered the fens defending unafraid.

Dragons abounded in those days far gone
wizards chanted many spells and magic.
Knight's legend grew by fearlessness alone,
poor peasant's miseries were but tragic.

Visions of Genevieve clouded his mind
whilst the great dragon Drockfus grew in strength.
Andrus knew to slay him was country's unwind
before Drockfus' size grew double his length.

Touching Genevieve's ribbon in his vest,
Andrus finally knew his one true quest.

Natures Assent

While crested waves crash, spraying stoned coastlines,
hair still flies wildly blown by stinging sand.
Branch's buds quake at winter's last gusting,
but songbirds peep knowledge from feathered puffs.

Spring creeps softly on pussywillow feet,
gently defying ice pellets barrage.
Yellow sprigs bring back battered down wishes,
newly grown grasslings return weathered hopes.

Forever snows fall, forcing entombment,
cramped up emotions screaming for stretching,
but when nature's assent nods every year,
comes torrid sun and coolest rains' patter.

The lone shack trembles at chilling howling,
but it's just bravado, dying flakes gasp.

Days of Future - Past

Just outside the photograph,
brushing the periphery of my vision
softly, breathlessly
as a feather, he was there-
comfortingly omnipresent.

Almost all-knowing but completely human
his quasi-presence cast a fog like blanket
barely touching my skin
like a cotton cumulus cloud,
tricking me into thinking I was free,
but covering me as thoroughly as a net
holding a fish struggling for oxygen on
the deck of life
never comprehending its' gills weren't
equipped for it.

In one instant the fog lifted-
filling me with pain and the false exuberance
of sliding back, this time into
the all enveloping water, at first warm and freeing,
all too soon a freezing void where my
only comfort was the knowledge
that once beyond the edge of the photograph,
once outside the periphery of my vision,
he had been there.

Wonderland

I Must Have Become Alice
Lately from Wonderland who has now
seemingly passed
through the looking glass.
A strange doublespeak has
replaced what I thought and
fervently hoped were truths.

In this strange new land
nothing means what is spoken
and the axis of reality
shifted.
Don't believe anything,
stupid child, this is Never Never Land.

Never trust, your own
truths are hubris,
the stuff in which pigs wallow,
the muck at lake's bottom,
a barnyard.
NEVER believe.

I Found Myself

I spied a lady alone and forlorn.
Sensing her problems were solved with great haste
I wended footsteps to help what was borne,
"Alas", she cried, "has my life been a waste?"

She sighed, "all I want are my aims to thrive
please listen and give me all your advice.
I need to find ways to fully revive
my life and loves which were once full of spice.

My figure and face were once very fair
my soul and life too fanciful and free.
I never gave others much of a care
and now my existence seems far at sea.

I was more selfish than any can say
did more harm than good and nothing is right."
My throat shut, I ran, the night had turned day,
myself I had seen with future's true sight.

Obsolescence

Listen well, beautiful young girls and pay close attention.
You are gorgeous, slim and your luminous smile lights
a room when you choose to flash it.
You are learning your power; the strength of a sideways
glance, the appeal of a wide-eyed gaze, the invitation
of a swaying hips walk.

You think you have it all but you know nothing of life.
Now you are 30 and are starting to come of age
and are learning well.
You really think you have it all.
Now you are 40. You look great. Only you notice some
wrinkles, sun blotches, a few pounds. You can cover it up.

You have gained wisdom.
You have most of it.
Now you are 50. Gee, you look good for your age.
Sometimes
you still turn heads.
Newly found security says you're the same.

You've learned most of life's lessons.
Now you are 60. You can't fool yourself any longer.
You're getting old.
No matter your education or accomplishments.
you're invisible and ignored,
but you know yourself.

Still comes the sting of knowing your completeness is
OBSOLETE!
(But WE know differently.)

Pandora

My name is Pandora, not Pan, not Pandy,
and most definitely not Pandy Pie.

My name is taken from
that ancient Greek girl
who opened the box of evils.

Did anybody call her "Pandy"?
REALLY!
I am an elegant looking
tortoise shell,
but not with the airy-fairy Aphrodite look
whose name these humans I let live
with me were bandying about.

(as if I were a plaything)
REALLY!

Now here they come with
that stupid looking rubber mouse on a string.

They like ME to jump around
and chase it as if I were an aberrant monkey.

I guess I'd better humor them.
(The things I do for my dinner.)
REALLY!

When will I get any respect?

Tattoo

The waxing and waning
of strong feelings etched
tatooed their indelible ink

could should would
we try again

Much more was the bliss
but how searing the pain
red hot words branded

could should would
we try again

but emotions remain
stronger than steel
whispering shrieks of why not

could should would
we try again

up and down
revolve and reverse

can shall will
we try again

The Air Sprite

When golden rays intrude vacuum's dense black,

while silence pervades mist's insulation,

drinking your sweetened wine I luxuriate,

an air sprite assured of affection's voice.

During midday's slashed streaming light,

When intensity heightens bright colors

I grow more aware and value your presence-

ever deepening roots and standing firm.

When gray tendrils invade ferocious hues

and gentle murmurs replace violent passions

again I drink sweetened wine and remember

how happy the air sprite stayed here

The Dress Shop

I am a dress shop,
well established,
(a euphemism for old,
and well-patronized for just
that reason.)
The people I have seen,

oy vey!

In the beginning
I was like the drab,
babushkaed women I served,
work, work, work, in the
new country where streets were
paved with gelt, ha ha!
The people I have seen,

oy vey!

Soon my address became "fashionable".
How can that be?
An address "is", it doesn't wear clothes.
These people,

OY VEY!

As the years went by
women became streamlined.
How can that be?
They don't work, but their faces look like
leather tanned and dried over bone.
This is fashion?
How can this be?
These people are walking clothes hangars,

OY VEY!

I have seen fresh faced, dimpled
young things swelled with pride
making the most important purchase
youth decrees, the prom gown,
young matrons ALL have a little black dress,
middle-aged women love Coco Chanel.
Old women buy expensive, drab colors.
How predictable,

OY VEY!

One day a silent, calm, bespectacled
old woman wearing a faded cotton housedress crept in.
Wrapped in a handkerchief were dollar bills.
Quarters, dimes, nickels,
pennies saved over years, eons.

She wanted the fanciest red dress
her money could buy.
I heard my clerk ask,
"For what occasion is this ?"
She answered, "a funeral"
and my clerk immediately offered
condolences,
but to my surprise
she brushed them away.

"I have been waiting
fifty whole years
for that nasty, old coot
to kick the bucket.
Nothing will keep me from
dancing at his funeral!"
The people I have seen,

OY VEY, OY VEY!

The Encounter

His smell, containing his cologne
and something much less definable
permeated my being.

At last peace, at last contentment.
Torment, begone; happiness, return.
My head hears the return of comfort,
sees the joy of being,
smells the absence of pain
as the whispers of consciousness
clang into shards of agony.

A single teaspoonful of instant coffee
signals the return of
yet another unwelcoming morning
to be endured......
alone.

The Farmer's Wife

Hot bread on table, gravy yet in vat,

fresh pork on carving board trimming off fat..

Sounds of tractor sowing, kids shouting glee

hoots hail the twilight from owls perched in tree.

Table laid and waiting, places set for four,

soft humming farmer's wife did it before.

Flames glimmer grating, children safe a'bed,

husband sits silently with nodding head.

She smiles and rises, brew's last cup of tea

gentles him with a kiss, slides up his knee.

Opens bleary eyes, smiles and gives yawning.

" Come sleep 'tis time, it's up soon 'ere dawning."

The Masquerade Ball

The quaint masquerade sways its beginning,
orchestral strains weave such harmonies fair.
Flourishing, each pair stately descending
using footsteps with more than common care.

Whirling and twirling masked dancers abound,
bubbling champagne, merry costumed revels.
Masks and fantasy uneasily mount,
Surrealness swells paranoia levels.

Faster and faster, flying hats, whisped hair,
the music forces frenetic movement.
As puppets on a string the dancers leap,
what pulls snares of disillusionment?

Nothing is .all that it pretends to be,
masks pretty and ugly staringly leer.
Distorted shapes like carnival mirrors,
cause spectrous beings to suddenly jeer.

Midnight comes when they begin to unmask.
Silence settles, movement stops, laughter rises.
Imagination done, they see simply friends,
not evil at all; what thought compromises.

Bridges To Tomorrow

I wanted to stay inside your embrace,
I wanted to hide my red tearstained face,
I wanted to feel your ten fingers trace
wantings and longings we couldn't erase.

Chorus

Rainbows can't grow over yesterday's dreams
and promises made in the sun.
Some things will crush
if we dare rush
building bridges in time yet to gleam.

I wanted to tell you how much I care
I wanted to hear things hanging in air
of wishes and hoping all that we dare
not spoken or whispered because we scare.

Chorus

Cause rainbows can't grow on yesterday's dreams
and promises made in the sun.
Some things will crush
if we dare rush
building bridges in time yet to gleam

We can't assume
things said in June
will carry us through to the end.
Remembering
gets in the way
of living the way it should be.

Chorus

Cause rainbows can't grow on yesterday's dreams
and promises made in the sun.
Some things will crush
if we dare rush
building bridges in time yet to gleam.

The Words Left Unsaid

In how many conversations are
words left unsaid; the juice, the substance,
the truth, the unfettered
REAL definition and delineation?
How many times do conversations end
prematurely;
so much of it left fallow
to molder and be left ignored,
untouched upon?
How I long to hear the nuances,
meanings, the secrets held in
the left-over verse.
WHY IS the must-be silence?
Where goes all the
nouns, verbs and adjectives,
the prose and poetry
of the hundreds, no thousands of times when
the meanings were discarded and diminished -
and the words were left unsaid?

We Go Dancing

We go dancing among the stars
whirling in Venus' embraces
glancing off the glowers of Mars,
hiding in bowers of laces.

Flying around faces in moons
trailing in Milky Way's guidance,
listening to celestial croons,
watching dreams and wishes enhance

Awake wind combs hair like your hand,
the sun warms me as does your kiss,
bird's song sweetly sings your command
and bids me find naught is amiss.

We go dancing among the stars
hiding in bowers of laces.

Life...A Masquerade

The wooden floors were decaying,
moldering, encrusted with the
ground in dust and dirt of
thousands of awe-stricken wannabes
and even more applause-bewitched actors
whose footfalls had unintentionally
worn and embedded their genuinely loved
boards with grime.

They crowded onto the stage
with the stars spilling out
of big, incandescent eyes.
Act, of course I can.
Sing, dance, mimic, just leave it to me.
Hope reigns.

My first big part,
but I'm only on standby...
never before have I wished anyone ill,
but, always the bridesmaid, never the bride.

And so the years go on,
every hope crushed,
every dream smashed.
Now each day beseeches the lead to die
with thoughts draped in cynicism.

Whatever happened, whatever became of
shining young faces laughing unbidden?
Masks melt into one, hardened and unsmiling.
Only in the unforgiving glare of footlights,
they morph into caricature, the painted -on smiles of
clowns.

Lollipops and Dandelions

One soggy, half unwrapped acid green lollipop,

and a straggle of moist, wilted dandelions

were the sacred momentos of a long forgotten love.

My love, my friend was an everpresent companion

stealing unwelcomed kisses

because he thought it was THE thing to do.

He didn't really want to.

Kisses were yucky, pointless things.

My mother and I made Rice Krispie candy

and I proudly shared it.

Then came the unnoticed void.

The preschool year had become summer.

Playing Right Along

Hide and seek, jump rope

a child's garden of verses

playing right along

get to school on time

earn A's with every subject

playing right along

married smiles assent

do exactly as you please

playing right along.

My Fine Cat

Hello there, my name is Jenny.
I met your kin named Millie.

She said you'uns were right nice
and you liked letters full of spice.

I cain't give you that,
but I'll try to tell you 'bout my cat.

I've had her nigh on 20 year,
And she'll not let you fear.

A better mouser ne'er did live,
bugs and rats she too will sieve.

Bats and possums stay away,
rodents all keep at bay.

We found a teensy kitten,
one paw big as a mitten.

Under the porch she did hide,
screamin' out a mouth so wide.

She don't come out
so old John made her pout.

He wriggled and did wiggle
(boy, did we giggle)

watchin' his butt
go through the cut

made in the porch that day.
He fished her out some way.

The like I've never seen,
old John and his queen

'cause the cat fell in love with him
like savior with cherubim.

To this day when he goes,
she cries like she seen crows,

And when he sits a while
that cat do smile,
AND IT STILL BE THE SAME
OLD JOHN AND HIS DAME!

41

She

She, ordinarily beautiful, poor,
wanting more, a fine lady wannabe

with liberated stubborness
born from generations struggling
only for their due
chose the flashing lights and drumbeat
music that was backdropped
by men yelling MORE!

It would be only for a few months until
damp wadded dollars
were saved, then a fine lady would
make a metamorphosis
struggling up through layers
of tacky sequins, cheap scent and sweat.

The years slid by smoothly,
without notice,
and the old bag lady on the corner
with her mouth slashed with red
straightens her question mark back,

musters fading energy,

and curtsies.

Fate

Fate, you are fickle, mostly I hate you.

You shone so brightly but for a moment

and I kissed your feet and thanked forever

praised the heavens and danced on my trials.

I felt happiness would forever be

and fell for your lies full force once again.

While I sang your songs and flew on the wind

you threw me rope and said 'go hang yourself.'.

Fate you are being a son of a bitch,

a lying cheat, a real piece of work,

but when the worm turns, it's you I will thank

and the stars will twinkle, hope will be mine.

The Iron Lady

My emotions lay naked,
each nerve rubbed raw.

Blood red achingly throbbing,
as I watch helpless, unable to move.

Watching the moths of decay
beginning to gather
around the festering sores
that have become my soul.

Bit by bit being forced
into a mold, an iron lady
my mind will not accept
I pretend, hence the sores.

Never will they heal
but in a perfect world
of which there are none.
Will I ever learn or
is this my fate?

The Tulip

The aura of unreality thickens
tasting of fungus and musty, damp rotting wood.
Will this thickening fog ever lift-
ever thick this malodorous muck
masked as atmosphere.

When can I breathe-expand my ribs;
where is the air, the sun, my life?
Under layers of this putrid morass I lie
or am I under the surface like a tulip bulb
biding its' time for a majestic head to unfurl.

Now I am what I choose to be,
here wading through a viscous pool
raising my head to the sun
choosing the light
hoping that with it comes the air and my life.

Usurping Dawn

I dreamed of you the other night
happiness fogged the clear window
I never saw brilliantine light
or heard breeze blow or felt it flow

I never saw suns' spilling gold
smelled fragrant newly mown grasses
with dandelion wine's air's bold
and intoxicating sasses

corona red paints lighted world
that's been frozen in shades of gray
moonshine's kingdom of starshine whirled
when it's domain lost battled fray

only you could usurp the dawn
and leave it's fine beauty to yawn

47

Rumors

Like an exotic lily oozing perfumed acid,

truth often is wrongly perceived.

Whether unknowingly or purposely

the tongue lovingly, longingly

wraps itself around what it wants

and loves.

The result rarely has much to do with truth,

what's that?

Like a sea sponge ready, no,

eager to absorb the most fetid,

decaying filth it can,

ears seek to hear what they want,

gaining perverse pleasure

from misfortune.

And Now!!!!

Trudging along, one foot after another,

dragging myself - forcing movement.

Throat drying quickly, rasps with each

painful breath of the arid, sulfuric air.

Once green and full of plenty,

the empty fallow lands are covered

by windswept sands, and I search.

Looking for signs of humanity,

a signal that I am not alone.

Ahh, could that be a windmill far away,

but no, it's a dry waterwheel, futility trying.

The nuclear barrenness took us by surprise.

Never had I envisioned the ending humankind

And I Dived

I looked in your eyes

expecting to see

the bottom

like I see the coins

in a wishing well.

I saw the deepest,

luminescent pools

ever envisioned and

I didn't wade or slip-

I dove in as deeply

as I could.

I never looked back,

finding shadings of hues

never imagined

or seen since.

Staying long

breathing your existence.

living our memories

feeling our essence.

When did I come up for air

and saw only vapors

of what should have been

but wasn't.

Once Upon a Time

Once upon a time, deep in the heart of me,
there was only myself, lonely for we.
Along came you, singing sweet lovely song.
Sonnets dripped off your tongue said I belong.

We drank summers wine and ate of the bread,
danced barefoot in grass and went where it led,
swam crystalline pools, thought ne'er of future.
Watched cloudy castles, lay long in rapture.

Autumn's fires with stinging breeze burned brightly,
signs of restlessness showed very slightly.
Before winters anger raged snow and ice,
you left me lonesome without thinking twice.

I cried to the sun and wept to the moon,
"could you leave me alone, scared and marooned?'
I picked myself up and thought once for me,
but never forgot when two ones were we.

Your Face

When last I saw your face somewhere,
the trees had turned gray and brittle.
The bread of which we had eaten
now became tasteless dust of clay.

What if yesterday's illusion
was a forgotten nightmare, a dream?
I have taken this path before,
but still it's new and frightening.

I know I should have called you back
but instead bade loving goodbye,
not throwing myself at your feet,
giving you peace you richly need.

Was that shooting star a comet
emblazoned by Aquarius,
the moon bowing his obeisance.
You, for one last time, waved your hand.

Storms

Lightening, thunder, hail and plague,
are naught when seen with eyes from within.

The roar of a tornado, the sting of sleet,
a curtain of monsoon, ice pellets in June.

Feverish rages of heat in March,
shivers and chill of a Maytime night.

The roar of disgruntled hurricanes,
the mewling of satisfied winds.

Pounding tsunami and hungering whirlpools
all pale in contrast to the storms from within.

A calm, sunny warm day is as rare as snow in July,
as are cool, still waters ceilinged by misty rainbows

and the chance to unstress with seamless sleep
still is naught when seen through

the eye of the storm from within.

Only One Star

Did you know you're my one star shining bright,
do you know I see your face in the moon
and make many wishes with all my might
to free myself from a self-made cocoon?

I want to spread my wings to fly without fear,
show my true colors and not have great shame,
bring what is too far to sit being dear,
to do all this gladly and not feel deep blame.

I want to soar with sweet breezes and sun,
run free with the deer and hide in dense trees,
swimming with mermaids and floating when done,
knit seaweed crowns and go home by degrees.

What must be said to one in a far land,
but I need breathe my fear and take a stand.

My Love

My dear, my love, my being,
can I say it well?

You are my life, my very soul,
you're in each breath I take.

Light of my life, day of my night,
just be all that you are.

I wonder where and what I'd be
without you in my life.

And may I say with no regret,
I wish it so forevermore.

Collections

I have gathered many things in my life:

laughter, frowns, fears and tears,

fleeting half smiles, the soul -piercing looks.

The gut-wrenching "I tried", knowing it's no good,

frustration, heartbreak, gloom and doom.

Hearty smiles, those phony emotion hooks.

Then honestly happy knowing I at least I tried,

satisfaction, pride, bile and trial.

But I was permitted to try,

letting my wings free to break as they may,

leaving my will to go wrong as it might.

Confusion, allusion, intrusion, illusion,

then clarity, reason and truth prevailed

as hope wished it would.

Life won and continues.

Ambling and stumbling

Ambling and stumbling along the

rocky path, watchful of my days,

reckoning on heartbreaking episodes

grown too many to count.

Feeling only the breeze comb my hair,

the suns' warmth on my skin,

lavender redolence bathes the mists

of a carefree and glowing awareness.

Too long thoughts had tormented an

otherwise logical, unshrouded,

unstinting being, thoughts growing

old, weatherbeaten, sorrowful,

suddenly vanished, making way

for emergent freedom, spacious

conciousness, air.

A decision made, more steady feet

traversed, content, where only nebulous

bits of the furious passions, fiery peaks

and valleys remained, but also days when

blossoms flourished, and sweet wine

was ours.

Back in the Day

Back in the day I was young and naïve

I thought being pretty would forever be

and old was a something caught by others

like people sunning themselves in the park.

Then came the age of loves' freedom and wine

when pleasure came sweet and too freely taken.

Swiftly swords slashed with payments made by pain

never occurring that costs were building.

Age glimpses more age, wisdom soothes,

tempering fiery reckless young passions.

Chances today may charge too high a price

but leave mem'ry honeyed more than before.

The Colors of Life

Gray, tan, shadowy black,
beige, brown, grayish mauve.
Dissonant chords forever clack,
on a barren, desiccated world.

One day, yellow, bright burnished red,
pink, sky blue, royal purple.
Melodies fine symphonies play in your head,
songs seemingly endless.

Without warning, it turns burnt umber,
melting into a pool of densest black
Songs turn to grating shrieks encumber
music once so fine and lasting.

Life is a balance, a juggling act,
of red and black, music and noise.
Still it remains a bitter fact,
we live for the pink and yellow waltz.

Come Fair Haired Minstrel

Come fair haired minstrel,
follow this goddess woman
who tantalizes your sweet
sleepy thoughts with redolent
flowers and sugared wine.

Come fair haired man,
she is whispering promised
paradise with sacred pleasures
and blood red lips,
enchanting your twilight musings
with sounds so fleeting
the angels envy them.

Come fair haired god,
enter this crystalline cave
and let her enthrall,
enticing dreamlike distant travels,
embrace her name, SLEEP.

Dragonflies hover

Dragonflies hover
bumblebees drone in late blooms
cicadas buzz dreams

lovers breathe longings
thrown back heads laughing nonsense
whispered sweet secrets

still water laps 'hush'
the pond fears summers demise
life's abandonment

The Corsage

Alone she sits, tightly holding memories.

Velvet, torn lace, a dried up corsage.

Once happy, thoughtless, once carefree,

remembrance hits with sabotage.

Quiet, calm, sheltered and alone,

will never be enough to nourish

peace interrupted with thoughts

that make a mind sing and flourish.

Who would think that girl dancing carefree

was the same woman worn, tired and alone.

She who tread merrily on countless hearts,

found a heart where games were stone.

Who lost, who won, the painful, useless joust.

The burned out man, unfulfilled and struggling,

or a woman so wounded she won't take a chance

on life, love or the joys she was juggling.

Veiled curtains and solitude is destined

for one's whose misdeeds won't be forgotten.

Through many years and silence, both wanting

fogged memory made dim; forgiving misbegotten.

Merry-Go-Round

Horses on the merry-go-round watch clowns
playing jokes, running around make pratfalls,
seemingly entranced by the myriad
of balloons of many colors and hues.

Tapping toes tenaciously, their manes fly
because they see their unheard angst felt,
feel the palpable timeworn hopelessness,
hear the singular sensation murmured.

"Nevermore be entranced by its beauty",
tattered spangles reinforce my resolve.
Clowns, comedians, funny men all,
hide despairing feelings inside hollow laughs.

I Felt the Yacht's Might

I felt the yacht's might slide into the dock,
It's mighty prow cutting through crested waves.
Shuddering halt with sails stopped billowing.
I wondered why I ever was wary.

Contentedly stretched arms to sun's last rays,
Viking captain poured ambrosia's scent.
The drink of the gods made it so heady,
Knowing not if I'm awake or asleep.

His smiling eyes caught starlight's first twinkle
As we dancingly embraced in lover's whirl.
Twirling and sighing the hours away,
Finally resting at dawn's first pale light.

Awakening sunburned on naked skin,
I all alone but dreamily happy,
Was my captain a sweet specter, a wraith?
But he appeared, the yacht performed magic!

Santa, Come Hither

Dear Mr. Santa, jes' what would YOU like,

I'm a red hot mamma and don't want no bike.

I bin real, REAL good and bin lookin' for gold,

Them dimonds too, the whole truth be told.

I saw a red car and boy did it shine,

Minks and sable make me feel jes' right fine.

Dear Mr. Santa, what clothes should I wear?

Somethin' real see thru and lacy and bare,

or silky that slips off right fast as crepe,

And if you want to, we'll shut that there drape.

Mr. Santa, if you be good to me,

You'll find lots of goodies under the tree.

Nothin' as stupid as cookies an' milk,

but your deepest dream or such of that ilk.

Boy think of all the things I can do,

By the way Mr. S., you forgot your shoe.

On A Clear Night

On a clear night I watch each twinkling star,
in night I study faces in the moon.
I think of things near and those very far.
I wish and hope I might be granted a boon.

One dark night I see a brilliant firefly,
But no, it's a candle's wavering light.
I reach out my hand to a breeze gone by,
It is grasped firmly, but not in my sight.

Soaring so high, my breath taken away,
How well do I fare, my bright shining light?
Where am I going, when along comes day?
Back down to earth with a wish shimmering bright.

Minds

With how many have I shared minds,

plumbing our depths finding we agree?

Then when upon starting to explore thoughts

both kindred and diverse he begins to flee?

With how many have I listened to laments,

endless woes, delights and continuing strife?

How universally often have I haltingly begun

thoughts to ears deaf, which cut like a knife?

Out of a darkened vacuum, an endless void,

shone a few stellar pinpoints of matchless light.

They said many things, the grandest of which

tell ME your mind, tell ME what you might.

So it went and one day (how unexpected),

one light stayed and shone much brighter than the rest.

Never had I known the name of contentment,

my bliss, my pain, my very, very best.

Then one day light began to diminish,

and I screamed the endless scream in vain.

The light grew dimmer and finally snuffed

the blinding light now veiled dark with pain.

Life continued, I walked as a robot,

mind and heart sealed in automatic drive.

So it went and one day (how unexpected),

a pinpoint of light stayed and helped me survive.

Little Boy

Little boy, little boy
with hair of gold and sun,
you ran and laughed, played ar
delighted just to be.

Little boy, little boy,
what terrors did you see?
Were you just another babe
or wired from the start?

Innocent young child,
you were a friend of mine.
Where did you come from
and why did you go?

Young man, young man,
with face so fair and finely mad
What horrors filled your mind
you made come true?

Young man, young man,
so kindly mannered and polite
Your face masked, your words li
how dared you be?

Handsome, kindly young man,
I thought you were friend,
But why did you come,
we're just glad you went!

Grown up man, you changed my life
for better and for worse.
What horrors have you wrought,
what terror did you bring?

Hearing heinous things you did
twisted mind and soul.
When they threw the switch
did you know things we knew,
you're evil and you're monstrous
and we're far better off.

Grown man, young man,
I'm glad you were a true friend not.
Why, why did vou come,
we're just glad you died!

Forever I'll ask,
but there's no answer,
just space
and a labryinth of riddles,
all asking

WHY?

The Computer

A computer says "I'm a dumb machine",
but we all know in different ways,
the infuriating, quiet frustration.
Evil incarnate, with your mind it plays.

Type one letter wrong, it decides to balk,
not moving one dot 'til you decipher and glean,
gleeful, evil, manic puzzles it finds
to turn your thoughts from serene to MEAN.

Harken, here's the one wrong move,
I'll lock up and here's a lesson I'll teach.
Don't mess with me you stupid mortal
Or (HA HA), I'll crash with your tears, you leech.

Inevitability

As I am swirled

through and around

iridescent radiance

tumbling gliding soaring

searing joy

permeates each pore

my mind looses

reason thought intellect fails

primal instincts

cannot comprehend

caution fear pain

as I am spiraled

downward

faster and faster

to the end.

Life's Illusions Lost

Long ago and very far away
when once upon a time came true;
where fireflies danced sprites airily flitted
when this magical, mysterious world was new.

Deep in the woods was fleetingly heard
distant strains of Pan's melodious mischance's.
Certainty said wood nymphs must hide
where mists of twilight met sunlight's enhances.

76

A visit was made to this magical place
by a sadder, wiser person who carried
not simple, careless, unrestrained years,
but time with the burdens and knowledge's married.

What was viewed was a tiny back yard,
two trees, straggly gardens and a few small yew.
Could this be where imagination ran wild,
where colors ran rampant and butterflies flew?

I never regretted life's lessons learned,
but remembrance brings thoughts, "Oh what a cost!",
not once to view through child's clear-eyed sight,
life's truest illusions, forevermore lost!

Somewhere

Someplace where forever has ended,
the bell tower has ceased to chime.
Somplace all the watches stopped ticking

and the hourglass's sand ran out.

Somewhere the sundial can't tell time

and the waterclock stopped dripping hours.

Somewhere through and beyond the looking glass

far along the yellow brick road

where surreal and empty space exists

love reigns supreme and in the center

appears

TRUTH!

Goodbye!

The day is so icy,

my fingers are painful.

Will you cease being,

childlike, irresponsible,

and be at least accountable

to whatever remains spiritual

in your soul?

Will you loose the menagerie

of spites, imagined insults,

perhaps your anger even,

keeping it off my back?

Walk away, just go,

and if the scents of

my perfume stay fresh

in your thoughts,

you made me go.

The Other Side Of Now

Where would I be without a now?

Would I be happy - warm - carefree?

I think of my sorrows and heartbreaks

they would never have seen day's break.

Embarrassment leaving scorched cheeks

heavy times heaved out the windows

cash always filling my pockets

ardure - suffering never known.

But then I'd never know heaven

the ecstasy and pain of you

the ins and outs of paradise -

that's the other side of now!

Fantasies and Foibles

Fantasies and Foibles,

We all need in life,

They help us develop

As we daydream through strife.

Other Books by P.F.P.Publishers.

More Books By P.F.P.

THE CROSS

Michael L. Schuh

Pieces of Existence

Joe Hartman

Tribute To A Songbird
Lela Cain

By
Poets World-Wide

Poems & Promises
A Tapestry of Dreams

William Garrett & Rochelle E Fischer

Windows of Light
Shining
With Love

Patricia Ann Farnsworth-Simpson

Born To Be a Rebel

Joanne Agee

Life's Carousel

Nita Wild
Patricia Ann Farnsworth-Simpson

"Joseph's Star"
or
Eternal Promise
"Poetry of God and Nature"

Christine R. Jussaume

Castle Of Ice

Daveda Gruber

A Blonde View Of Life

Daveda Gruber

MIKE and JOE

Michael L Schuh

Embroidered Limericks

Patricia Ann Farnsworth-Simpson

DOWN THE ROAD WE CAME
"Treasured Memories"

Poems and stories of yesteryear and beyond
Robert Hewett Sr

The Last Trail Ride
"Story Poems of the Old West"

Robert L. Hewitt

83